The Joy of Not Giving A Damn

The Joy of Not Giving A Damn

Katie Simpson

Copyright

The Joy of Not Giving a Damn
© 2025 Katherine Simpson

Published in the United States by Ember & Oak Press, Montana. For inquires visit www.katiesimpsonbooks.com.

ISBN: 979-8-9931490-3-5
Cover design by Katie Simpson
Printed in the United States of America

First Edition

Disclaimer

This book is a work of nonfiction based on the author's personal experiences, opinions, and humor. Certain names, timelines, and identifying details have been changed to protect privacy. Any resemblance to actual persons, living or dead, is coincidental. The events and interpretations described reflect the author's perspective and should not be construed as objective fact. This book is not intended to provide medical, legal, mental health, or professional advice. Readers seeking such guidance should consult a qualified professional.

Dedication

For Ken.

My partner in crime, my comic relief, my protector, my love. You are proof that love after the fire is not only possible, but hilarious.

This book wouldn't exist without you, or at least, it wouldn't be nearly as funny.

Preface

Why This Book Exists (and Why You'll Probably Laugh Anyway).

If you read my memoir *My Own Damn Table*, you know the backstory. I stopped begging for a seat at tables where I was never really welcome and built my own instead. That was about survival, reclamation, and figuring out who I was after years of dysfunction.

This book? This one is about what comes next. The joy. The freedom. The unapologetic decision to stop giving a damn about things (and people) that were never worthy of my energy in the first place.

For most of my life, I gave way too many damns. I worried about family drama, church politics, workplace nonsense, and the peanut gallery's opinion of every choice I made. I apologized for existing too loudly, too honestly, too much. It was exhausting.

Then I realized something radical. Damns are a limited resource. If you hand them out to everyone who demands one, you'll have nothing left for yourself. The real power move isn't in giving more, but in choosing fewer—carefully, intentionally, joyfully.

This book is not a manual on bitterness, not a rant against humanity, but a love letter to boundaries, humor, and peace.

It's about finding joy in the chaos, laughing at the absurd, and refusing to apologize for living on your own terms.

And yes, you'll hear a lot about Ken. My husband, my comic relief, my occasional bodyguard, who is always up for an adventure. He has a way of reminding me that life is supposed to be funny, even when it's hard. And sometimes *especially* when it's hard.

So if you're tired of guilt trips, toxic people, and the endless pressure to shrink yourself for someone else's comfort, welcome. This is your invitation to laugh, breathe, and join me in the fine art of not giving a damn.

Before we can stop giving a damn, we have to know *who* we've been giving them to. Life is full of characters, gaslighters, guilt-trippers, control freaks, and chaos enthusiasts , each with their own brand of crazy. This book is your survival guide to spotting them early, setting them straight (or setting them free), and protecting your peace like it's designer merchandise.

Because once you learn to save your damns for what actually matters, life gets a whole lot lighter, and a whole lot funnier.

Acknowledgments

Most authors thank their mentors, editors, or cheerleaders here. I'd like to thank… dysfunction.

To every gaslighter, guilt-tripper, manipulator, and hypocrite who crossed my path: congratulations. You gave me an endless supply of material. Without you, this book might have been a polite pamphlet on stress management instead of a comedy of survival.

To my animals. Yes, even the chickens who scream at Ken like he owes them child support, thank you for reminding me that joy often looks ridiculous. You've been my therapy, my distraction, and sometimes my best punchline.

To my friends, the ones who know me in all my sarcastic, unapologetic glory: thank you for laughing with me, for never asking me to shrink, and for showing up without judgment or fine print. You're proof that family is chosen, not assigned.

And to Ken, always Ken. Thank you for turning life into a sitcom I actually enjoy being in. For standing beside me in every storm, for making me laugh when laughter felt impossible, and for showing me daily that real love is equal parts loyalty, patience, and a perfectly timed one-liner.

Finally, to the reader. THANK YOU. You picked up this book, which means you're ready to stop giving so many damns. My hope is that these pages give you permission to breathe easier, laugh harder, and choose joy on your own terms.

Because in the end, that's all I really owe anyone. The truth, the humor, and the reminder that life's too short to waste on the wrong damns.

TABLE OF CONTENTS

Chapter 1: Spotting Gaslighters in the Wild

Of all the characters you'll meet in life's circus, gaslighters are the trickiest. I didn't wake up one day magically fluent in spotting gaslighters. I wish. It took years of confusion, self-doubt, and more than a few ugly-cry bathroom breaks before I realized the problem wasn't me; it was them.

Twenty years ago, nobody called it "gaslighting." TikTok therapists weren't packaging red flags in neat little carousels. Back then, you just said someone was an asshole and tried to move on. Or you shoved the mess into your emotional junk drawer and prayed it didn't pop open when company came over.

The behavior hasn't changed. Assholes just got rebranded.

Gaslighters don't look like villains. They're not twirling mustaches or stroking cats in a lair. They're your boss, your parent, your spouse, or that Facebook cousin who starts every insult with, "I'm just being honest." They are not honest. They're cruel with a halo on.

If you've ever walked away from a conversation thinking, *Wait, am I losing it? Did that really happen?* Congratulations, you've met one. And if you're like me, your first instinct was probably to second-guess yourself. You tried to be nicer, calmer, more understanding. You explained yourself seventeen different ways, convinced that if you found the right combination of words, they'd finally get it.

Newsflash: they don't. That's the point.

Gaslighters excel at turning their screw-ups into your problem. They'll say something nasty, and when you call them on it, suddenly you're "too sensitive." Or they'll deny what they said while you're standing there holding the receipts, sometimes literally.

Like the boss who denied a whole conversation while flipping through the notebook where I'd written his exact words. Sir, you are holding the evidence. That's like being caught with chocolate on your face while swearing you've never seen a brownie.

Or the family member who told me I "needed thicker skin" after a brutal holiday ambush. My response? "Or maybe you should stop poking it." Not well-received, but oh, it felt good.

And don't get me started on the line, "Everyone agrees with me." Who the hell is everyone? Usually two bitter people and a dog that doesn't even like them.

The reality is that gaslighting works. Especially if you grew up in dysfunction where you were trained to keep the peace at all costs. Once they make you doubt yourself, you're clay in their hands. They don't even have to be good liars, just persistent.

There is hope. Once you see it, you can't unsee it. Gaslighting thrives in the dark. Flip on the light, and suddenly it looks less like wizardry and more like a toddler with a broken wand demanding applause.

That's where not giving a damn comes in. Gaslighters count on you to over-explain, apologize, doubt your own memory. But the moment you mentally — or out loud, if you're feeling spicy — tell them to fuck off, the spell breaks. You remember you don't owe them your reality, your peace, or your damn sanity.

Once you stop playing their game, the illusion crumbles. They're not masterminds. They're just magicians without a trick, demanding applause for smoke and mirrors. And honestly? I don't give a damn.

Chapter 2: Red Flags & Other Party Tricks

Gaslighters are just one species in the larger zoo of dysfunction. Let's talk about the rest of the herd.

Once you've spotted their tricks, it's time to widen the lens. Because red flags come in every shape, size, and emotional hair color. Some people walk into a room and bring light. Others walk in and suck the oxygen out like a broken Shop-Vac. You don't need a psychology degree to tell the difference. One bad Thanksgiving, three terrible bosses, or a single HOA meeting is usually enough to make you a red-flag specialist.

Now, let me be clear. I'm not a therapist. I don't have a DSM tucked under my arm or a license to diagnose. What I do have is lived experience, sarcasm, and a finely tuned bullshit detector. And let me tell you, once you start noticing these types, you'll see them everywhere.

Some are obvious.

- The narcissist who treats every conversation like it's a press conference about their greatness.
- The drama queen who turns paper cuts into medical emergencies.
- The passive-aggressive "complimenter" who could drop a horse with the poison in their tone.

Others are sneakier. They show up in workplaces wrapped in khakis and a name badge.

Case in point. I once worked for a manager who actually said to me, straight-faced, *"Sometimes you have to teach a lesson by making it hurt so bad they don't forget."*

Excuse me? That's not leadership. That's villain-monologue material. Imagine telling your employees, *"Hey, I'm here to crush your spirit, but don't worry — it's for your own good."* I should've reported him to HR, but knowing corporate, HR probably would've given him a plaque.

What people miss about these red flags is that they're not hiding. They wave their dysfunction proudly, like it's the Macy's Thanksgiving Day Parade. And if you're not paying attention, they'll drag you onto their stage, hand you a script, and expect you to play along in their drama.

Here's how it usually plays out:

- They demand loyalty while offering none.
- They spin lies so confidently you start to wonder if you're the crazy one.
- They thrive on chaos, because as long as you're dancing to their tune, they don't have to face their own garbage.

Whether it's gaslighters, guilt-dealers, or garden-variety drama magnets, the goal is always the same — pull you into their chaos so you can't see clearly. Recognize the pattern once, and you'll start seeing it everywhere. It's emotional quicksand with a smile.

And if you grew up in dysfunction like I did, you're especially vulnerable. You normalize red flags. You explain them away, laugh them off, or worse you take responsibility for fixing them. (Newsflash: you can't fix someone who enjoys being broken. They'll fight you for their right to stay toxic.)

But here's the good news. Once you learn to spot the red flags, everything changes. You stop asking, *What's wrong with me?* and start realizing, *Ohhh, the problem isn't me — it's them.*

My turning point came when I realized that manager wasn't brilliant, scary, or even worth fearing. He was just pathetic. A man-child with a title, mistaking cruelty for leadership. Once I saw him clearly, I stopped giving him my power. I did my job, but I didn't let his poison seep into my bones.

That's when I learned the ultimate red-flag response isn't panic. It's detachment.

And sometimes, it's two little words: *not today (aka fuck off).*

Not always out loud (though everyone should try that at least once). Sometimes it's internal. Refusing to argue, refusing to defend, refusing to dance when they play their song. That quiet *not today* will mean *fuck off* louder than shouting.

Remember, you're not crazy. You're not broken. You're just dealing with people who mistake chaos for personality.

And once you see them clearly, they stop being dangerous. They just look… ridiculous.

Red flags aren't scary once you stop pretending they are. Call them what they are, roll your eyes, and move on.

That's the joy of not giving a damn.

Chapter 3: The Family Circus

Ah, family. The people who are supposed to love you unconditionally, support you through thick and thin, and make the holidays magical. Unless, of course, they don't.

Some families are less *Leave It to Beaver* and more Cirque du Dysfunction. Picture it - Dad as the strongman (but instead of lifting weights, he throws emotional punches), Mom as the magician (making love disappear), and siblings juggling loyalty depending on who holds the spotlight. Welcome to the dysfunction circus. Popcorn not included.

Growing up, I didn't need a ticket to the circus. I lived in the main ring. Every holiday, without fail, my father found a way to turn what should've been celebration into combat training. He had a sixth sense for when the turkey was carved, the gravy was poured, and the room was finally settling into that rare, cozy silence. That's when he'd pounce.

And his favorite target? Me.

He'd unleash an outburst, berating me in front of everyone like I was the evening's entertainment. When the dust settled and everyone was too stunned (or too cowardly to intervene), guess who got blamed for "ruining Thanksgiving"? Yep. Me. As if my mere existence had the power to sour the cranberry sauce.

The worst part wasn't his behavior. It was everyone else's silence. Some laughed nervously. Some stared at their plates like the mashed potatoes might save them. Some tried to change the subject. Nobody ever said, "Hey, maybe stop berating your daughter over dinner rolls." No, the family circus needs performers and apparently, I was the clown.

That's the cruel trick of family dysfunction. When it's strangers, you can walk away. When it's your father, your wiring gets scrambled. The people who are supposed to love you unconditionally end up teaching you that love is conditional. That love is based on obedience, silence, or sacrifice. And that messes with your head for years.

Holidays are prime time for this circus. Thanksgiving, Christmas, weddings; these are all the big stages. Passive-aggressive comments passed along with the stuffing. Guilt trips disguised as "tradition." Manipulation hidden behind "but we're family." Dysfunction loves an audience.

If you've ever left a holiday gathering needing therapy, wine, and maybe an exorcism? Congratulations, you've been to the show.

DNA isn't a hall pass to abuse. Just because someone shares your last name doesn't mean they get a lifetime membership to your soul. If family gatherings leave you bleeding every time, you have every right to stop buying tickets to the circus.

And yes, people will talk. They'll call you selfish. Cold. Ungrateful. They'll wring their hands about "family loyalty." Let them. Because you will be free.

And sometimes, that's the quietest, most powerful "fuck off" you'll ever deliver. Not slamming doors or screaming matches (though those have their place), but a simple:

- "No, I'm not coming this year."
- "No, I'm not discussing politics, religion, or forgiveness on your terms."
- Or silence. Simply choosing not to volunteer as the evening's punching bag.

Family should mean love, respect, and safety. Contrary to popular belief, you do not have to put up with the abuse. You get to define family for yourself. And if that means skipping Thanksgiving for peace and wine in pajamas? Cheers. I don't give a damn.

Chapter 4: Churches, Bosses, and Other Cult Leaders

Not all cult leaders wear robes, wave sage around and chant in the desert. Some wear three-piece suits. Some carry clipboards. Some stand behind pulpits with fake smiles plastered on their faces. And some? Some sit in corner offices tracking bathroom breaks like it's the Hunger Games.

The common thread? Control.

I know this one up close. As a young, abused wife and exhausted mother, the church was supposed to be my refuge. It should have been a place to breathe, to heal, to feel safe. Instead, it became another arena of expectation and shame.

I'll never forget standing in front of puffed-up church leaders declaring, *"God has called you to serve."* Meanwhile, I was hanging on by a thread. I was sleep-deprived, stressed, emotionally wrung out. I had nothing left to give. But apparently God still needed me to chair a potluck or babysit the congregation's drama.

When I finally whispered "no," they didn't hear it as a boundary. They heard it as rebellion. I wasn't tired, I was "disobedient." I wasn't protecting myself, I was "turning away from God." They made sure I knew the punishment too: eternal damnation. Apparently, Hell is reserved for people who skip casserole duty.

That's not faith. That's extortion with hymnals.

Once you've seen it in one place, you start to notice the same playbook everywhere: churches, workplaces, HOAs, PTA meetings. The leaders may look different, but the tactics are always the same:

- **Fear**: "If you don't obey, bad things will happen."
- **Guilt**: "If you really cared, you'd do what I say."
- **Shame**: "Good women don't say no."
- **Isolation**: "We're your true family — anyone outside is dangerous."

Sound familiar? That's not divine wisdom or management brilliance. That's control. The church slaps God's name on it, the office slaps "company values" on it.

I once worked for a company that was "faith-based." Nothing wrong with faith. Except this wasn't about faith. Every morning, before you were allowed to start your actual job, you were required to stand in a circle and pray with the team. Not invited. Required. Refusing wasn't really an option unless you wanted to be labeled difficult or, worse, godless. Not only was this illegal, it was surreal. Coming straight out of religious captivity, it set off every alarm bell in me. I hadn't escaped one system of control just to clock into another one disguised as a paycheck. Work should be about your skills, not about proving your devotion on company time.

A paycheck doesn't entitle anyone to own you. Neither does a pulpit. Neither does some smug neighbor waving an HOA covenant like it's scripture.

So yes, sometimes the most spiritual thing you can say is *not today.* Consider this door closed. Not to God, but to the gatekeepers who confuse obedience with holiness. Sometimes the most professional thing you can say is *not today* to a boss who mistakes cruelty for motivation.

Because the biggest lie these so-called leaders tell — whether they're waving a Bible, a performance review, or a homeowner's manual — is *you need us.*

Leaders who demand loyalty but give nothing back aren't leaders, they're parasites. The second you stop buying their nonsense, they wither. And you? You get your joy back.

Chapter 5: "No" is a Complete Sentence

If I had a dollar for every time I explained, justified, or over-apologized for saying no, I could've bought my own island, named it Boundaries, and charged toxic people admission.

No is a complete sentence. Period. It doesn't need a dissertation, an apology, or a tearful TED Talk. Just two letters and done.

Of course, I didn't learn that lesson the easy way. The first time I said no to my ex-husband, he struck me in the back of the head so hard I saw stars. One moment I was daring to claim the tiniest scrap of autonomy, and the next I was flat on the floor, my head ringing. I was stunned, terrified and confused.

In that stunned moment, I realized something that has stayed with me ever since. *No* is powerful. My refusal provoked a violent reaction, proof that "no" wasn't weakness. It was power.

When you grow up in dysfunction, *no* feels like a crime. You're conditioned to believe saying no makes you selfish, ungrateful, or downright unlovable. Add in a little religious guilt, and suddenly every no feels like you're flipping God off while marching into Hell. No wonder it's so damn hard to say.

That conditioning leads straight into the *Over-Explaining Olympics*:

- "I'm so sorry, I can't make it, but I have this other thing, and then my kid has practice, and maybe next time I promise…"
- "No, I can't stay late at work, but if you *really* need me, I'll cancel dinner, skip sleep, and run on fumes. Totally fine!"
- My personal favorite - apologizing to others for their mistake. (Why are we like this?)

Every extra word you pile on is an engraved invitation for people to negotiate your boundaries. Toxic people hear explanations the way sharks smell blood.

Here's what I eventually figured out. People who only "love" you when you say yes don't actually love you. They love access to you.

That's why sometimes "no" isn't enough. Sometimes you need the deluxe version: *fuck off.*

Not out of rage but out of clarity. It's the verbal equivalent of slamming the door on a salesman who refuses to stop sticking his foot in. It's saying, *I've explained myself enough. This conversation is over.*

The first time you say it, your whole body might shake. The guilt shows up like expired takeout; heavy, sour, and not worth it. But if you ride it out? Oh, baby. By the tenth time, it feels like freedom. You stop handing out yeses like Halloween candy and start treating them like what they are: a gift. And not everyone deserves it.

No is your lock. Not giving a damn about their tantrums? That's your security system. Together, they buy you peace.

So, no. I don't owe you my time, my energy, or my soul.

Chapter 6: The Guilt Hangover

So you finally did it. You said no. Maybe even dropped a solid *fuck off.* You stood tall, set the boundary, walked away with your head high, feeling powerful and free…

…and then the guilt kicked in like tequila on an empty stomach.

Welcome to the guilt hangover.

I grew up apologizing for everything from talking too loud, walking too loud, existing the wrong way. If air took up space, I probably would've apologized for inhaling too much of it. I became a one-woman apology machine, cranking out "I'm sorrys" for things that weren't even my fault.

When you're trained that way, guilt becomes autopilot. You don't even notice it anymore, it just hums in the background like bad elevator music. Saying no felt dangerous. Terrifying. Like the second I declined something, people would stop liking me, stop loving me, or punish me. So I said yes. Over and over. Until I was drained, resentful, and wondering why everyone else was thriving while I was barely holding it together.

Then one day, I had a boss who saw right through me. She wasn't perfect, but she was kind, genuinely kind, with a streak of spunk. One afternoon she looked me in the eye and said, *"Katie, you need to stop apologizing for everything."*

I blinked, because at the time, apologizing felt as natural as breathing. Stop apologizing? For *everything*? That sounded like walking on water. But she didn't stop there. She told me that saying no wasn't weakness, it was maturity. That it was okay to draw a line and stand on the other side of it, unapologetically.

I almost cried on the spot. No one had ever told me that before. My entire life had been built on the idea that "good girls" apologize and bend until they break. And here was someone, in authority no less, telling me I didn't have to beg permission to exist.

That conversation planted a seed. Maybe guilt wasn't my moral compass. Maybe it was just the leash other people yanked whenever I tried to walk away.

The ugly truth about guilt is it's a manipulative little bastard. It whispers like a bad ex who won't move out. *You're selfish. You hurt their feelings. They'll hate you now. You're ungrateful. You're just like them.* Same script every time, designed to pull you back in line.

But guilt isn't truth. It's a smoke alarm that goes off when you toast a bagel. Loud, panicked, and completely wrong.

So how do you survive the guilt hangover? You ride it out. You remind yourself why you said no, and you fight the urge to backpedal. You comfort yourself. Snack on something, pet the damn dog, distract your brain, until the buzzing in your chest quiets. The first time feels like treason. By the fifth, it feels like jaywalking. By the tenth, saying no barely registers.

People who love you don't weaponize guilt. The ones who do weaponize guilt? They're not protecting you. They're protecting their access to you.

So the next time guilt slithers back in, whispering the same tired lines, pour yourself a drink, throw on sweatpants, and smile.

Guilt isn't truth, it's just noise. And the joy comes when you finally stop giving a damn about the noise.

Chapter 7: Protecting Your Peace Like It's Prada

Peace is underrated. People act like it's whipped cream on a latte. Nice if you can get it, but not essential.

Wrong. Peace isn't whipped cream. Peace is oxygen. Peace is sanity. Peace is bliss. Peace is the designer bag of emotional health, and you better guard it like it's a limited-edition Prada everyone's grubby hands are trying to snatch.

But I didn't always know that.

Toward the end of my first marriage, peace wasn't even a concept. I was so deep in survival mode that I dissociated just to make it through the day. I felt like I was watching my life play out from inside a fishbowl; detached, observing, not really living. On the outside, I was functioning. On the inside, I was gone.

When you live in constant flight mode, you miss everything. Conversations blur. Faces become wallpaper. Laughter feels foreign. Sunsets pass you by. Your child's smile becomes background noise. You're in the room, but not in the room. And it robs you blind mentally, emotionally, physically.

It took years to recover. Years to trust that calm wasn't just the silence before the storm. Years to believe peace wasn't a trap. But when it finally came? It was life changing.

The first time I truly felt peace, I thought: *Is this what people live like all the time?* I could breathe. I could sleep without nightmares. I noticed the little things. Morning light through the curtains, birds at dawn, ridiculous synchronicities that made life feel magical. Butterflies weren't just bugs anymore; they were tiny miracles I'd been too numb to see.

And once peace showed up, gratitude followed. Gratitude brought love. And suddenly, life wasn't about survival anymore. It was about living.

The hard truth is peace is expensive. It costs you people. It costs you obligations. It costs you being liked by everyone. It costs you the version of yourself who bent until she broke. Once you realize that, you stop treating peace like an accessory and start treating it like oxygen. You guard it with everything you've got.

So no, I don't owe anyone my peace. Not family who want to drag me back into the circus. Not churches that guilt me into servitude. Not bosses who think burnout is a badge of honor.

Peace is non-negotiable.

And if anyone doesn't like it? They can take a number.

Peace is oxygen, not an accessory. If it costs me peace, it's off the rack. I don't give a damn how 'important' it's supposed to be.

Chapter 8: Integrity — The Only Pillar You Really Need

When your whole world collapses — family, marriage, church, career — there's only one thing left standing that actually matters: your integrity.

Not your reputation. That can be shredded in seconds by louder voices and nastier lies.

Not your approval ratings. Those swing depending on whose ass you kissed last.

Not even your so-called "legacy," because let's be real; half the people telling your story will twist it for their own benefit.

What you do have, the only thing no one can take unless you hand it over, is integrity. That quiet, stubborn knowing that you told the truth, lived authentically, and refused to sell your soul just to make someone else comfortable.

And let me tell you, integrity is expensive. Sometimes painfully so.

I learned that during a custody battle so vicious it felt like war. People said such horrific things about me that I started to believe them. I thought, *If I heard this about someone else, I wouldn't like her either.* Even my own attorney bailed, saying the way I was being portrayed made me "too toxic" to represent. Imagine being so slandered that your paid defender decides you're bad for their brand.

Yet, I refused to break.

I went into the final court battle alone. No lawyer. No backup. Just me. They beat on me until I was nearly dead inside, but I never bent the truth. I never abandoned myself. And when it was over, I walked out of that courtroom with my head held high.

And here's the part that still makes me laugh. I wore a miniskirt out of religious spite. That may not sound like much, but it was my rebellion. My not-so-subtle "kiss my ass" to every holier-than-thou hypocrite who thought they could shame me into silence.

I made it to the entryway, stopped, and (in my head and probably on my face) told everyone in that room exactly what they deserved: *fuck off.*

And then I left. I was done.

What nobody tells you about integrity is people who are invested in dysfunction hate it. Because once you start living by it, they can't control you anymore. You won't lie to protect them. You won't play the scapegoat. You won't clap for the emperor's new clothes just because they told you to. And that drives them wild.

They'll call you stubborn. Difficult. Bitter. Unforgiving. Translation: you stopped playing their game, and now they're itchy about it.

Integrity is why you can sleep at night. It's why you can look in the mirror and say, *I didn't betray myself today.* It's the one thing that outlasts gossip, lies, and smear campaigns.

So when people demand you bend, compromise, or cover their mess with your silence? The answer is simple. Tell them to *fuck off.*

Not because you're cruel, but because your soul is not up for negotiation.

At the end of the day, reputations fade. Gossip dies. People forget. But integrity? Integrity is the only thing that lasts and it costs me exactly zero damns to keep it.

Integrity is where you start but it's not where you stop. Once you've rebuilt your life on truth, you realize integrity alone isn't enough. You still have to stand in it. You still have to protect it. That's where power comes in; not the loud, ego-driven kind that bullies use, but the quiet, grounded kind that comes from finally knowing who the hell you are and refusing to hand that power away again.

Let's talk about what reclaiming that power actually looks like and how to do it without losing your humor in the process.

Chapter 9: How to Reclaim Your Power (Without Losing Your Humor)

Power gets a bad reputation. We're told it's loud, aggressive, maybe even selfish. That having power means taking it from someone else.

Wrong. Real power isn't a performance. It's peace. It's that calm, grounded confidence that comes from knowing who you are and no longer needing anyone else's permission to exist.

When you grow up in chaos, you confuse control with power. You think being loudest wins. Or you think power belongs to the people who hurt you, because they always seemed to have the upper hand. But here's the truth I wish someone had told me years ago: **power isn't what they have over you — it's what you take back from them.**

You reclaim your power the moment you stop explaining yourself to people committed to misunderstanding you.

You reclaim your power when you stop trying to convince the unconvincible.

You reclaim your power every time you choose peace over the urge to prove your worth.

Reclaiming power doesn't require a speech, an audience, or a perfectly timed mic drop (though those are fun). It's quieter than that. It's deleting the message without responding.

Blocking the number. Unfollowing the guilt trip. Walking away mid-conversation when someone starts rewriting history. It's not passive, it's powerful restraint.

It's not revenge either. Revenge still ties you to them.
Reclaiming power is freedom.
It's saying, "You no longer get to decide how I feel about myself," and meaning it.

Let's be clear, this isn't about pretending you're unbothered. You'll still get angry, hurt, triggered. You'll still replay conversations in the shower. You're human. Power isn't the absence of reaction; it's mastering the *recovery time*.

You'll know you've reclaimed your power when things that used to ruin your day now barely ruin your coffee.

When their opinion still stings for a minute but no longer dictates your mood for a week.

When you start laughing instead of spiraling.

That's power.
That's progress.
That's peace.

And humor? Humor is your crown jewel.

Because nothing confuses manipulators more than being met with calm laughter instead of panic. They expect your tears, your anger, your need to defend. They do not expect a smirk and a sip of coffee.

The ultimate flex isn't "winning" the argument. It's not needing one.

It's knowing the truth, holding your integrity, and finding your joy anyway.

The Double Standard of Power

Here's the confusing double standard. When men reclaim their power, they're called confident, assertive, strong. When women do it, we're labeled difficult, emotional, uncooperative, even "bitchy."

A man can raise his voice in a meeting and its passion.
A woman raises hers, and it's "attitude."
A man sets boundaries and he's decisive.
A woman sets boundaries and she's "not a team player."

It's exhausting, isn't it?

The world teaches women to make their strength palatable. To smile while saying no, to soften truth with pleasantries, to apologize before speaking up. We're conditioned to be digestible, not powerful.

But here's what I've learned. You can't heal while staying small. You can't reclaim power while tiptoeing around fragile egos. You don't owe anyone comfort while you find your voice.

For some reason when a woman stands firm, it threatens people who rely on her compliance. They'll call it arrogance, stubbornness, even sin because it forces them to confront the fact that they no longer own her.

So, reclaim your power loudly if you need to.
Calmly if you prefer.
Laughing if that's your style.
But reclaim it all the same.

Because you don't need to be "likable" to be powerful.
You need to be *authentic.*
And that's far scarier to people than aggression ever was.

Quick Power Reclamation Practice

Try this simple self-check whenever you feel your peace slipping:

Ask yourself:

- Am I explaining myself to someone who already decided I'm wrong?
- Am I trying to be liked more than I'm trying to be honest?
- Am I staying small so someone else feels comfortable?
- Is this worth my peace, or just my pride?

Then breathe.
Choose quiet confidence over chaos.
And if all else fails, pour a cup of coffee, smirk to yourself, and whisper:

"You don't live here anymore."

That's power.
That's freedom.
And that's the joy of not giving a damn.

Chapter 10: Not Damaged, Just Caffeinated

The uncomfortable truth is we're all broken. Some of us are cracked down the middle, some chipped on the edges, and some look like clearance-rack plates glued back together with Elmer's glue. That is the reality of life.

But broken doesn't mean worthless. Broken doesn't mean damaged goods. Broken just means you've lived through some shit and you're still standing. Honestly, I think the people without scars are the suspicious ones. Who gets through life without breaking at least once? Robots, that's who.

And if anyone knew how to crank up the shame dial, it was the religion I grew up in. Everything was sinful; thoughts, words, clothes, what you drank, who you looked at, how you breathed. I remember reading church material that claimed premarital sex was basically second only to murder. Murder. As in stab someone, or make out in the back seat, same penalty. What the actual hell?

And don't even get me started on coffee. I was taught if I so much as touched a cup, I'd basically combust on the spot. Funny thing. I'm still here. Still caffeinated.

Here's where it gets rich. While I was terrified of eternal damnation over a latte, it wasn't unusual to see the bishop's wife sipping Starbucks or heading out for an R-rated movie night. Apparently, the rules only applied to the peasants.

Nothing says "holy" like condemning caffeine while your own kitchen smells like caramel macchiato.

That's the problem with systems built on control. They thrive on making you feel defective while their leaders break the rules behind closed doors. You end up thinking you're damaged goods because you slipped, while the people preaching perfection are out there sinning with whipped cream on top.

Here's what I know now:

- Your upbringing doesn't define you. If it did, I'd still choke on guilt every time I said "hell" while mowing the lawn.
- Your circumstances don't define you. If they did, I'd still be trapped in a bad marriage, convinced casserole duty was my holy calling.
- Other people's opinions sure as hell don't define you. If they did, I'd be a walking scarlet letter instead of a woman writing books and laughing with her husband about chickens that stalk him.

We're not fragile figurines in a gift shop. We're thrift-store furniture. We are solid, a little scratched, maybe missing a knob, but still standing and ready for another round. And thrift-store furniture has character. Nobody brags about their brand-new IKEA nightstand, but they'll rave about the beat-up old dresser that's been through hell and still holds socks.

So let's call it like it is:

- You're not damaged. You're experienced.
- You're not broken. You're seasoned.
- You're not baggage. You're carry-on with extra legroom.

Perfection is a scam. None of us are flawless. We're all limping toward the finish line with duct tape on our souls, pretending we know what we're doing. That's not failure. That's humanity.

You're not damaged. You are a limited edition. And if anyone tries to put you on clearance? Smile, sip your coffee, and don't give a damn.

Chapter 11: Humor as Survival Skill

I talk to myself all the time. Mostly because I need good advice. And let's be honest, I'm the only one I can trust to give it straight. Some people think it's weird. I call it strategy. Because sometimes your best defense in life isn't a long speech, a dramatic walkout, or even a well-timed *fuck off.* Sometimes your best weapon is humor.

Humor is survival. It's how you crawl out of hell without smelling like smoke. It's how you flip the bird to shame, turn pain into punchlines, and disarm people who thought they had you cornered.

And sometimes? Humor shows up in the most ridiculous places.

Take the time I was at the grocery store, fantasizing about telling off one of my enemies. You know the kind of imaginary fight where you rehearse your lines, land every comeback, and drop the mic so hard you're sure Hollywood will call? Yeah, that one.

Except I wasn't just thinking it. I was acting it out. Hand gestures. Facial expressions. Full dramatic performance down the frozen food aisle, like I was auditioning for "Most Possessed Woman of The Year."

I didn't realize until I noticed people staring. People parted like I was contagious, giving me the whole damn aisle to myself. Mothers pulled their kids closer. Husbands backed up like, *Oh hell no, not today.*

And you know what I did? I laughed so hard I cried. Right there, clutching a bag of baby carrots, mascara running, shaking with laughter in aisle seven. What could've been humiliating became one of my favorite stories. Because humor has a way of rescuing you. Even from yourself.

If you let it, bitterness eats you alive. Humor spits it out, dresses it up, and sells tickets to the show. People expect survivors to be broken, quiet, maybe "inspirational" if you play it safe. They don't expect sarcasm sharp enough to slice steel. And that's exactly what makes humor such a weapon.

It's rebellion. It's defiance. It's survival with a punchline.

So yes, I talk to myself. I laugh at myself. I embarrass myself on the regular. But that's the point. If I can laugh at me, then no one else gets to use it against me.

Humor is my rebellion, my defiance, my survival skill. I'm not bitter. I'm hilarious. And that's why I don't give a damn.

Chapter 12: The Joy of Not Giving a Damn

There comes a day when you wake up, stretch, sip your coffee, and realize… you don't give a damn anymore.

Not about their approval.
Not about their gossip.
Not about the peanut gallery whispering from the cheap seats of your life.

And let me tell you, the first time you feel it, it's glorious. Like taking off a bra after a 14-hour day. Like canceling plans you didn't want to go to in the first place. Pure bliss.

For me, the biggest revelation came with the church crowd. In my humble opinion, they were the absolute worst (at least where I came from). They strutted around on Sunday mornings pretending to be holy, but the second service ended, they were spreading lies, gossiping about you, and feasting on your trauma like it was the latest Netflix series. These are the folks who pray for you with one hand and sharpen the knife with the other.

For years, I thought I had to stay. I thought God would strike me with lightning if I dared to leave. I thought the doors of heaven would slam shut if I didn't show up, smile, and let myself be judged week after week.

But one day, I had an epiphany. God wasn't the problem. The assholes pretending to represent Him were. And I didn't owe them my time, my obedience, or my silence.

So I sat down and wrote the most fabulous "fuck off, you ruined my life with your lies" letter the world has ever seen. It wasn't polite. It wasn't flowery. It wasn't subtle. It was cathartic. Every truth I'd swallowed for years finally poured out on paper. When I signed my name at the bottom, I felt lighter than I had in decades.

I wasn't afraid anymore. I didn't care if they whispered. I didn't care if they lied. I didn't care if they clutched their pearls and declared me a heathen. I was free.

That was the day I stopped giving a damn. And once you taste that kind of freedom, you never go back.

Because here's the reality. Your damns are limited. They're a finite resource. And wasting them on people who thrive on your pain is like handing out full tanks of gas to arsonists. Not everyone is entitled to your energy. Not everyone deserves a damn.

So now, I save mine. My damns go to people who show up with love, respect, and no strings attached. They go to Ken, who makes me laugh daily. They go to my animals, who demand attention but never judgment. They go to the friends who know the real me and cheer her on.

My damns are limited edition, and I spend them carefully. Everyone else? Sorry, you're out of luck. And I couldn't be happier about it.

Chapter 13: Love After the Fire

Love after chaos doesn't look like the movies. There are no violins swelling in the background. No dreamy montages of beach walks while jazz plays softly in the distance. No dramatic declarations under the stars.

Real love? Real love is everyday comedy. It's inside jokes, eye rolls across the room, tag-teaming chores, and laughing until you can't breathe over something ridiculous. It's messy, protective, and absolutely yours.

That's what I have with Ken. He's not just my husband. He's my partner, my co-conspirator, my comic relief, and (when necessary) my bodyguard. He's the quiet-but-don't-piss-him-off type. You know the kind: doesn't say much, but when he walks into a room, people part. Not because he's loud, but because he doesn't need to be. His presence does the work.

One of the funniest (and most epic) things Ken ever did was meet the religious crowd on my behalf (still makes me laugh just thinking about it).

The day the religious crowd came to the house, they thought they were about to put me "back in my place." Instead, they got Ken. At the door. In nothing but his underwear… and a gun belt.

He didn't say a word. He didn't have to. He just stood there, calm as can be, letting silence do all the heavy lifting while those church folks scrambled to figure out whether they'd walked into a morality play or a Tarantino movie. They got an eyeful they'll never forget. And as they turned to scatter away, Ken quietly said, *"Thanks for stopping by. Bless your hearts."* It was the icing on the cake.

That's Ken in a nutshell. Silent but devastating. Protective without being controlling. Hilarious without even trying. He doesn't waste words. He lets his presence, timing, and occasionally inappropriate wardrobe choices say it all.

After everything I'd been through (the chaos, the manipulation, the constant eggshell walking) finding this kind of love felt like learning a new language. At first, it was uncomfortable. Peaceful love feels suspicious when you're used to war. But over time, I realized the truth. Real love isn't about constant passion or drama. It's about safety. It's about laughter. It's about knowing someone has your back no matter what.

Ken is the person who laughs with me daily, rolls his eyes when my chickens destroy the garden, and stands in the doorway half-dressed to scare the hell out of hypocrites who thought they could intimidate me. That's love after the fire. Not flowers and violins — underwear and a gun belt.

And honestly? I'll take that any day.

Love after the fire isn't about perfection. It's about peace. It's about laughter. And it's about looking at each other, grinning, and saying "*We're happy and we don't give a damn who approves.*

Chapter 14: Exit Strategies With Style

By now, you've figured out that not giving a damn isn't just a mood. It's a lifestyle. A philosophy. A survival skill. But like any good skill, delivery matters.

Sure, you can storm out of a room and slam the door and sometimes, that's exactly what the situation calls for. But the most satisfying exits are the ones with flair. The ones you replay in your head later like the highlight reel of your own personal blooper comedy.

For me, the greatest example will always be The Great Pajama Breakout.

Ken was stuck in a long-term recovery unit after a surgery and the place was a circus. The staff was useless, dismissive, incompetent, and about as helpful as a screen door on a submarine. He was miserable, lonely, and starving—as if Jell-O cups and air qualified as a complete food group.

Then, late one night, my phone rang. Ken whispered like a prisoner in a spy movie: "Please come get me."

That was all I needed to hear.

I threw my bathrobe over my pajamas, grabbed my keys, and sped over like I was pulling off a heist. I marched through the front doors without stopping at the desk because hesitation is how you get caught. Rule number one of jailbreaks: look like you belong. Rule number two: if you don't look like you belong, at least look like you'll ruin someone's week if they stop you.

I found Ken sitting in his bed, half-dead and me, fully furious, said, "We're leaving. Now." He gave me that oh God, she's really doing this look, but also smirked like, *this is why I married her*.

I loaded him into a wheelchair like it was a low-budget action movie. We were halfway down the hall before the staff realized I wasn't joking. Nurses started yelling like I'd stolen state secrets, demanding I "return him" as if my husband were overdue library property.

I stopped, spun around in all my pajama-clad glory, and announced, "He's not a library book! He's my husband, and you're not the boss of me! I'm taking him home!" Then, because subtlety has never been my strong suit. I added, "You can't have him anymore!" before snatching every pamphlet on display like a deranged raccoon and tossing them into the trash with dramatic flourish. The lid spun for what felt like an eternity. Pure poetic justice in stainless steel.

Then I pushed that wheelchair with the squeaky wheel straight through the exit doors like it was the finale of a very cheap action film. Forget Thelma and Louise, this was more like Bonnie and Clyde if Clyde had an IV and Bonnie wore Target flannel.

The best part? No one could stop us. The staff scattered like pigeons in a Walmart parking lot. Ken was laughing, I was laughing, and for the first time in days, he looked alive. We burst into the parking lot like fugitives making the big getaway. Except instead of a sleek escape car, I had a Honda Civic with half a tank of gas and stale French fries under the seat.

And you know what? He healed faster, better, and happier at home than he ever would have in that hellhole. To this day, he tells everyone about the night I staged his escape. Apparently, it cemented my reputation as "a little crazy." Personally, I call it stylish.

Not giving a damn doesn't always have to be loud or vulgar. Sometimes it's quiet. Sometimes it's funny. Sometimes it's delivered while wheeling your half-broken husband out of captivity at midnight in pajama pants.

Style isn't about the outfit (though plaid flannel pajamas do scream authority). Style is about delivery. It's about reclaiming space for yourself and the people you love and doing it with enough flair that no one ever forgets it.

So yes, slam doors when you need to. Smile sweetly when you want to. Wheel your man out of captivity if the situation calls for it. But whatever you do, do it with style.

Because people remember style.

And mine? Pajamas, defiance, and the joy of not giving a damn.

Chapter 15: Filling the Void (Without More Dysfunction)

So you've done it. You've set boundaries. You've said no. You've cut the cord. You've told people to fuck off (maybe in French, maybe in flannel pajamas). And now… silence.

What no one warns you is that when you finally clean house, you're left standing in a very empty room. No chaos. No manipulation. No guilt trips. Just quiet. And if you've lived in dysfunction long enough, quiet isn't peace. Quiet is suspicious.

That's when the void shows up.

And the temptation is strong to fill it with something, anything. A rebound relationship. A toxic friend. A soul-sucking job that keeps you busy enough to forget you're lonely. Chaos feels like home, even when it's poison.

I know, because I tried filling the void every way possible.

First attempt: hobbies. That's what normal people do, right? Hobbies. So I bought supplies, fired up Pinterest, and gave it a go. Spoiler: I am not a crafty person. I ended up with glue in my hair, paper stuck to the counter, and projects that looked like kindergarten art gone wrong. If Martha Stewart saw my work, she'd issue a restraining order.

Second attempt: fostering animals. Noble idea. Except I wanted to keep them all. Every scrappy cat, every sad-eyed puppy, every creature that sneezed in my direction. I wasn't fostering. I was auditioning for *Animal Hoarders.*

Third attempt: fitness. Because apparently endorphins fix everything. Yoga, Zumba, whatever the trendy class was. The problem? I'm not built for exercising. I'm uncoordinated, I trip over my own feet, and I hate sweating with the fiery passion of a thousand suns. Picture a drunk flamingo doing interpretive dance. That's me. After nearly concussing myself in a cardio class, I retired from fitness.

Finally, I stumbled into the real answer. Two tiny adorable Chihuahuas. Ridiculous. Demanding. Convinced they own me (and honestly, they're not wrong). But they gave me joy in a way crafts, chaos, and kale smoothies never could.

Ken, of course, pretended he didn't like them at first. Said things like, "They're your dogs," and "Don't get them used to sleeping in the bed." Two weeks later, he was baby-talking them like royalty as he tucked them in between us. The same man who fixes tractors and chops firewood now sings lullabies to six pounds of fur. I just sip my coffee and pretend I don't see it. Because honestly, it's the cutest damn thing in the world.

That's the thing about the void. It feels terrifying because it's unfamiliar. But if you don't rush to fill it with more dysfunction, eventually it fills with things that actually make you laugh, breathe, and feel alive. For me, it was Chihuahuas. For you, it might be painting, gardening, road trips, or binge-watching trash TV without guilt.

The point isn't what you choose. The point is that you get to choose.

And when you finally do? That's the ultimate freedom.

Because I'd rather trip over a Chihuahua than over someone else's chaos. That's the joy of choosing what fills my life and not giving a damn about the rest.

Chapter 16: Freedom is Awkward (and Amazing)

Nobody tells you that freedom can feel... weird.

After years of dysfunction, chaos, and control, you expect freedom to feel like a Hallmark movie complete with fireworks, sparkles, choirs of angels. Instead, freedom can feel awkward, like standing in a grocery aisle realizing no one's watching and you can pick whatever you want.

Freedom is glorious, yes. But it's also awkward as hell.

The first time you realize you're allowed to make your own decisions, you start second-guessing everything. Stay up late? Sleep in? Spend money on yourself? You catch yourself asking permission, from no one. Silence feels suspicious. Joy feels undeserved. Sometimes you'll even throw your own shoe just to hear the chaos you're used to.

And then there are the awkward-but-hilarious moments that remind you freedom doesn't look polished.

Take The Lawnmower Incident.

Ken, bless his patient soul, decided to teach me how to use the zero-turn riding lawnmower. It sounded simple enough: sit, steer, mow. But you should know by now that "simple" and I aren't on speaking terms.

I climbed on like I was about to qualify for NASCAR. Ken gave me very detailed instructions. I caught maybe half of them. Then I cranked that machine to full throttle and tore off like a lunatic.

Within minutes, I was flying in circles across the yard, laughing like a maniac, mowing down grass and dignity at the same time. And then, because chaos is my specialty, I took out half the fence. Boards splintered. Grass sprayed. And me? I was laughing so hard I literally peed my pants.

Ken just stood there, arms crossed, shaking his head with that look that said, *This is my life. This is my wife.*

Was it awkward? Absolutely. Embarrassing? Oh, 100 percent. But was it fun? Hell yes.

Freedom is messy. You'll make dumb choices. You'll screw things up. You'll break fences, overspend, buy plants you'll kill in a week, and eat ice cream straight from the carton at 2 a.m. But the beauty is those mistakes are yours. Not forced on you. Not guilt-tripped into existence. Yours.

In captivity, even your mistakes belong to someone else. They'll punish you for them, use them against you, twist them into proof you're unworthy. In freedom, your mistakes are just part of living.

Eventually, the awkwardness fades. You stop flinching at silence. You stop asking invisible permission. You start laughing at the mess. And one morning you'll wake up, sip your coffee, look out at your lopsided fence, and think: *This is my life. It's weird. It's messy. It's mine. And I fucking love it.*

Freedom doesn't have to be polished. It just has to be real. Crooked fences, bad mowing skills, and all. And that's where the joy lives.

Chapter 17: Building a Life That Feels Like Yours

Once you've cleared the chaos, cut the cords, and reclaimed your peace, you're left with a big, terrifying, and beautiful question...

Now what?

For years, your whole life revolved around surviving other people's storms. You got so used to dodging lightning bolts that when the sun finally came out, you didn't know what to do with it. Standing in the light feels amazing but also disorienting.

That's when it's time to stop reacting and start creating. To build a life that doesn't just look good on the outside but actually feels like yours. And spoiler alert; it probably won't look Pinterest-perfect.

Take the time Ken and I decided to go wine tasting. I stress *one* time because let's be real, we are not "sophisticated wine people." But we thought, why not? Free samples, a little adventure, maybe some romance.

At stop number one, I was already far more interested in the cheese than the wine. Because honestly, who doesn't love cheese? Wine is fine, but cheese is forever.

By stop number two, Ken had gone full Larry the Cable Guy with a wine glass — swirling it around, sniffing dramatically, nodding like he knew what "oaky undertones" meant. Meanwhile, I was calculating how many cheese cubes I could sneak without looking like a raccoon at a buffet.

By the end, we were $200 in wine debt, Ken was drunk and charming every stranger within five feet, and I was the designated driver wondering how "free samples" turned into "we need a second mortgage."

Was it classy? Not even close. Pretty? Absolutely not. Fun? ABSOFUCKINGLUTELY.

And that's the point. Building a life that feels like yours isn't about curating picture-perfect moments for Instagram. It's about finding joy in the mess, laughing at the chaos, and saying yes to experiences that don't make sense but make you feel alive.

For us, that looks like pizza "dinner parties" where we serve food straight from the box on paper plates. Sometimes our miscommunications are so ridiculous they turn into comedy sketches we still laugh about. Chickens screaming at Ken like he's their husband. And the occasional ill-advised wine tour. None of it's glamorous. But all of it is ours.

Because building a life that feels like yours isn't about perfection. It's about authenticity. It's mismatched mugs, backyard chaos, Chihuahuas ruling the couch, and moments that wouldn't impress anyone else but mean the world to you.

And that, my friend, is the ultimate *vindication.* A life designed by you, for you, with zero apologies and even less concern about who approves.

So no, it doesn't look like a glossy magazine spread. It looks like wine hangovers, paper plates, and laughter until your sides hurt.

It may not be perfect, but it's mine. And that's why I don't give a damn what anyone else thinks.

Chapter 18: Life's Too Short Not to Laugh

When you finally stop giving a damn about appearances, something magical happens. Life gets funny again. Not the fake kind of funny where you laugh to keep the peace, or chuckle politely because everyone else is. Real funny. The kind that makes you snort, cry, and wonder if you just wet your pants. (And sometimes, you do.)

For me and Ken, our life is a constant blend of love, chaos, and… chickens. Yes, chickens. Because at some point, we thought raising them would be wholesome — fresh eggs, rustic farm vibes, Pinterest-worthy cuteness.

Here's what no one tells you about Chickens. They poop everywhere. I mean *everywhere.* On the deck. In the garden. On your shoes. In your soul. They do not respect fences, coops, or human dignity. They are tiny feathered anarchists, and they will destroy everything you hold dear.

We have a rooster who genuinely thinks he's a dog. Call his name, and he comes running like a Labrador, chest puffed, tail feathers flying, ready for action. Then there's Ken's stalker hen. This one particular chicken has decided Ken is her soulmate. She follows him everywhere — to the yard, the shop, the fence line. She waits for him like a scorned lover and screams at him when she's mad. (Which is often. She's got standards.)

And the destruction? Don't even get me started. The yard? Gone. The garden? Obliterated. The deck? Looked like a battlefield. If you've never seen a flock of chickens take down a flower bed, imagine a gang of drunk toddlers with shovels and no adult supervision. That's about right.

And yet... I love them. Because in the middle of the chaos, they make me laugh. Every. Single. Day. The rooster-dog routine, Ken being screamed at by his feathered stalker, the sheer audacity of these birds tearing apart everything we've built, it's pure wholesome comedy.

That's the lesson, really. Life's too short not to laugh. We survived the fire, we rebuilt, we found peace and now we get to enjoy the absurdity. Chickens pooping on the deck? Funny. Chihuahuas running the house like mob bosses? Hilarious. Ken standing in his underwear and a gun belt scaring off church people? Iconic.

Because the best moments aren't curated. They're chaotic, messy, unplanned, and absolutely ours.

So if anyone doesn't like my chickens, my chaos, or my laughter?

I just don't give a damn because I'm busy living my best life.

Chapter 19: The Fine Art of Losing Your Sh*t

Sometimes you just lose your shit.

You try so hard to be calm, reasonable, the "bigger person." You breathe. You count to ten. You tell yourself, *don't take the bait.* You practice self-control like it's your side hustle. And then, BAM. One comment too many. One controlling tone. One smug look. And suddenly you're done.

The rational brain checks out. The filter leaves the building. And what's left? A feral, unhinged version of yourself who looks suspiciously like you but wilder — like your inner caveman finally clawed its way out.

And honestly? Sometimes that's exactly what you need.

Let me share a story. We call it the infamous Flower Bed Incident.

Ken and I once had an argument over — wait for it — how to water the flowers. Not finances, not parenting, not anything high-stakes. Flowers. Ken was mad I wasn't listening to his instructions. I was mad he was telling me what to do. Neither of us was budging. Tensions rose, voices escalated, and then something in me just snapped.

I stomped over to the flower bed, yanked those poor plants straight out of the ground, and — with all the righteous fury of a woman possessed — declared, *"Problem solved!"*

Ken froze, eyes wide, watching his beautiful flowers get ripped out like an HGTV horror show. He stared at me like I'd just summoned the spirit of Bigfoot. Me? I was triumphant. Arms crossed. Daring him to argue now.

Looking back, I was behaving like a complete lunatic. But at the time? Oh, it felt glorious.

What surprised me most was once the storm passed, we laughed about it. Hard. Ken still teases me about "that one time you ripped out the flowers like Bigfoot." What used to feel like shame now feels like affection for that story. Because it wasn't about flowers. It was about all the frustration I'd swallowed finally busting loose — messy, ridiculous, human.

That's the fine art of losing your shit. It's not pretty. It's not graceful. But sometimes it's necessary. When you've been trained to suppress, to stay small, to swallow your anger — letting it out, even in absurd ways, is liberation.

Losing your shit doesn't have to destroy everything. Sometimes it just clears the air. You scream, you cry, you rip out a few petunias. Then you laugh, you breathe, and you move on. And maybe it even becomes a story you tell years later, smiling because it shows how far you've come.

So yes, sometimes I will lose my shit. I'll cry in grocery stores, rip out flower beds, and deliver lines only exhaustion could produce. And I'm not apologizing for it. Because perfection is overrated.

The real art is learning to laugh at yourself afterward. And finding someone like Ken who laughs with you, not at you.

So here's my advice. Lose your shit once in a while. Do it with flair. Do it with full commitment. And when it's over, pour a glass of wine, look at the carnage, and laugh.

Sometimes losing your shit is the most honest thing you can do. And the joy is learning to laugh about it instead of giving a damn.

Chapter 20: The Things (and People) I No Longer Apologize For

For most of my life, "sorry" rolled off my tongue like a nervous tic. Sorry for talking. Sorry for laughing too loud. Sorry for being in the way. Sorry for existing. If oxygen was rationed, I probably would've apologized for inhaling too much of it.

And people loved it. Because apologizers are easy to control. Keep them guilty, keep them small, and they'll never question your power.

But somewhere along the way, I snapped. I realized apologizing for being myself was killing me. And I stopped.

So here's the short list of what I no longer apologize for:

1. Bullies.
I have a zero-tolerance policy for bullies in any shape or form — corporate, church, family, playground adults. For years, I let them push me around because I thought saying no made me "mean." Now? I don't tolerate them. The second they show their stripes, I'm out. Or, if necessary, I'll say it plain: *fuck off.*

2. My personality.
I used to tone myself down. Be quieter. Softer. Nicer. I was told I was "too much" — too sarcastic, too blunt, too direct. Guess what? I am too much. Too much for small minds.

Too much for weak egos. Too much for people who only feel big when I make myself small. And I'm done apologizing for it.

3. My boundaries.
If I say no, that's it. Not an invitation to negotiate. Not a cue for guilt-tripping. No is no. And I don't apologize for walking away from people who can't respect it.

4. My joy.
Laughing too loud. Loving Ken openly. Spoiling my Chihuahuas. Taking ridiculous delight in chickens that destroy my garden. I used to hide my joy because people called it "silly" or "selfish." Now I flaunt it. Joy is rebellion. And I will never apologize for it again.

5. My peace.
If someone threatens my peace, I don't care who they are — family, boss, friend, preacher — they're gone. Peace cost me too much to hand it over cheaply. If you don't like my boundaries? *Fuck off.*

Apologizing for who you are is just another way of giving away your power. And I'm fresh out of power to hand over.

So if you don't like me? If my humor's too sharp, my boundaries too firm, my freedom too loud? That's not my problem anymore.

Take me or leave me.

But if you choose to leave? Don't let the door hit you on the way out.

Because I don't apologize for being me. Not anymore. And the joy is, I don't give a damn who disagrees.

Chapter 21: Dumpster Couture & Other Fashion Statements

I have a confession. Fashion isn't my thing. Never has been, never will be. And at this point in life? I don't care.

For years, I thought I was supposed to care. Magazines, church ladies, Pinterest boards, and even well-meaning coworkers all had the same message: *Dress better. Look polished. Don't you want people to respect you?* Meanwhile, I'm over here just trying to tolerate socks for more than thirty minutes before I feel like I'm being strangled from the ankles down.

Shoes? Overrated. Socks? Torture devices. If I could go full Fred Flintstone year-round, I would.

And sure, I've tried. Every so often, I make a good faith effort to "improve my wardrobe." I scroll through online shops, load up a cart, click buy now, and convince myself I'm transforming into a classy human being. The clothes arrive, I try them on, and for a hot minute I think, *This is it. This is my new style.*

Fast-forward six months, and those same clothes are in the giveaway pile because — surprise — I never wore them. They hang in my closet like guilt trophies, silently mocking me while I reach for the same ratty sweatshirt and leggings. Eventually, I donate them, swearing I'll never waste money again… until I do.

My real fashion sense? Dumpster Couture. Whatever's clean, comfortable, and closest to the bed wins. Sometimes it matches, sometimes it doesn't, and sometimes it looks like I got dressed during a fire drill. Ken has raised an eyebrow more than once, and my response is always the same. *Don't look at me. Problem solved.*

And don't even get me started on "special occasion" dressing. I've walked into weddings and family gatherings in outfits that made people tilt their heads like confused golden retrievers. Apparently, jeans and a hoodie aren't considered "formal wear." Who knew?

Here's the irony. For someone who couldn't care less about clothes, I have a full-blown obsession with makeup, hair care, lotions, and perfume. Do I wear it? Rarely. Do I keep buying it? Absolutely.

I have no fewer than twenty different blushes in my bathroom drawer. Twenty. All in slightly different shades of pink and peach, just in case I suddenly decide to become a beauty influencer at fifty. My stash of body lotions could moisturize an entire village. My perfume collection could fumigate a department store. And don't even get me started on hair products. I own more bottles than an actual salon.

I call it *trying.* Ken calls it *hoarding.* He's probably right, but I like options.

I will line up my little army of products… and then walk out of the house barefaced, smelling faintly of chickens, in leggings with holes in them.

My proudest fashion statement of all time? Grocery shopping in pajama pants and my bathrobe. Zero shame. If you see me in Walmart looking like I just escaped a bunker, hair in seventeen directions, socks optional — know this: I am thriving.

Want to wear Crocs with socks? Do it. Want to live in leggings that have seen better days? Go for it. Fashion isn't in the fabric, it's in the attitude.

Because confidence isn't about heels and Spanx. It's not about labels or "what's in season." Confidence is rocking whatever's clean, laughing at yourself, and daring people to care. Because I sure don't give a damn.

Chapter 22: Redefining Family

Family is supposed to mean love, respect, and safety. It's supposed to be the soft place to land, the people who show up no matter what, the circle that holds you together when life falls apart.

But let's be honest, sometimes it's not. Sometimes "family" is just a group of people who happen to share your last name and feel entitled to your loyalty while giving you nothing but chaos in return.

I learned the hard way that blood doesn't guarantee loyalty. It doesn't guarantee kindness. It doesn't guarantee truth. Growing up, "family" often meant front-row seats to my humiliation. They were the chorus backing my father's outbursts, the silent witnesses who looked away while the circus burned, or the very people joining in to spread gossip and lies.

For years, I thought I had to accept it. I thought being a "good daughter" meant showing up, smiling, sacrificing, and swallowing my pain for appearances' sake. I thought walking away made me selfish, cold, ungrateful.

But eventually, I realized something radical. I get to decide what family means.

And when I stripped it down, here's what I found. Family is not defined by DNA. It's defined by love. By loyalty. By laughter. By people who don't weaponize your scars or turn your trauma into entertainment.

For me, family looks like Ken. He's my partner, protector, and co-star in every ridiculous story we've ever lived through. The man who will stand in the doorway in his underwear and a gun belt, scaring the hell out of hypocrites without saying a word. The man who makes me laugh until I can't breathe and never once uses my vulnerability against me.

Family looks like my animals. My ridiculous Chihuahuas who think they run the house. My chickens, chaotic little anarchists who scream at Ken like he's their husband. They may destroy my deck, but they've never lied about me, never manipulated me, never told me I was "too much." They just love me — unconditionally, messily, loudly.

Family looks like the people I've chosen. Friends who show up with humor, honesty, and no judgment. The ones who celebrate my wins, sit with me in my losses, and don't expect me to shrink so they can feel bigger. The ones who hear my sarcasm, my raw honesty, my *fuck offs,* and laugh because they get it.

Family can also mean silence. Walking away from the ones who couldn't or wouldn't love me the way I deserved. Refusing to keep paying admission to the family circus. No longer handing out invitations to people who only show up to throw knives.

I don't apologize for redefining family. I don't apologize for cutting ties with blood relatives who were toxic. I don't apologize for protecting my peace at the cost of their approval.

Because family isn't who shares your DNA. Family is who chooses you, every damn day, without keeping score.

Family isn't who you're stuck with, it's who you choose. And if anyone doesn't like my version? Too bad. I don't give a damn.

Conclusion: Living Unapologetically

Living unapologetically isn't about being perfect. It's about being free. It's about finding the joy in everyday life, as chaotic as it is.

For years, I thought freedom meant earning approval from family, from church, from bosses, from anyone who seemed to hold power over me. I thought if I apologized enough, bent enough, shrank enough, I could finally be "enough."

Turns out, that's the trap. The more you contort yourself for other people, the more they demand.

So I stopped.

I stopped apologizing for breathing too loud.
I stopped justifying every *no.*
I stopped handing out my peace like parade candy.
I stopped wasting my precious damns on people who thrived on my pain.

And when I stopped? Life opened up.

Not in a polished, Instagram-perfect way, but in a messy, hilarious, beautifully human way.

Because here's what unapologetic living actually looks like:

- Laughing so hard in the grocery store people think you're possessed.
- Ripping flowers out of the ground in a rage and later laughing about it like Bigfoot on a bender.
- Breaking Ken out of a recovery unit in your pajamas while the staff yells behind you.
- Being screamed at by chickens who think they own your husband.
- Wearing pajama pants to Walmart like it's the Met Gala.
- Declaring your *fuck offs* with flair — whether whispered in your head or shouted in the doorway.

Unapologetic living is peace. It's integrity. It's joy. It's choosing your people, your animals, your laughter, your messy-but-perfect life. It's deciding that if something costs you peace, it's too damn expensive. It's knowing your no is enough. Your truth is enough. *You* are enough.

And no, it won't always be graceful. Sometimes you'll lose your shit. Sometimes you'll cry. Sometimes you'll pee your pants on the lawnmower. But it will be real. It will be yours.

So when the gaslighters circle, when guilt slithers back in, when the peanut gallery whispers, when the world demands you shrink, remember this:

You don't owe them a single apology.
You don't owe them your peace.
You don't owe them a damn thing.

The only thing you owe is to yourself: to live out loud, laugh too hard, love fiercely, and never again apologize for who you are.

Living unapologetically isn't polished, but it's mine. And if anyone has a problem with that? I'll be too busy laughing and not giving a damn.

Author's Note: If You're Still Healing

If you're still in the thick of it, the crying, doubting, overthinking, the "what the actual hell is my life" part — take a breath.

You're not behind. You're not broken. You're just in progress.

Healing isn't linear. Some days you'll feel unstoppable, and other days you'll wonder if you've learned anything at all. That's normal. That's growth hiding in the mess.

You might still answer the phone for people you swore you'd block. You might still apologize for things that weren't your fault. You might still lose sleep replaying what you wish you'd said. That doesn't make you weak, it makes you human. Every boundary starts wobbly before it stands firm.

And eventually, one day, you'll notice something small, your shoulders aren't clenched. Your chest feels lighter. The noise fades. You'll laugh again. Not the polite kind, but the ugly, soul-deep kind that bubbles up from relief. That's when you'll know you're coming back to yourself.

Don't rush it. Don't judge it. Just keep choosing yourself in small ways from the coffee you love, the peace you crave, the "no" that protects your sanity. One choice at a time, one day at a time, you'll build your freedom.

And when you finally get there? When the chaos quiets and you realize you made it through?

Laugh. Because damn, you earned it.

You're not just surviving anymore.
You're living unapologetically.

And I'm cheering for you!

-Katie

www.ingramcontent.com/pod-product-compliance
Lightning Source LLC
Chambersburg PA
CBHW070534130626
46555CB00003B/1411